O'REILLY®
Strata
Making Data Work

Learn how to turn data into decisions.

T0256956

From startups to the Fortune 500, smart companies are betting on data-driven insight, seizing the opportunities that are emerging from the convergence of four powerful trends:

- New methods of collecting, managing, and analyzing data

- Cloud computing that offers inexpensive storage and flexible, on-demand computing power for massive data sets

- Visualization techniques that turn complex data into images that tell a compelling story

- Tools that make the power of data available to anyone

Get control over big data and turn it into insight with O'Reilly's Strata offerings. Find the inspiration and information to create new products or revive existing ones, understand customer behavior, and get the data edge.

O'REILLY®

Visit oreilly.com/data to learn more.

50 Tips and Tricks for MongoDB Developers

50 Tips and Tricks for MongoDB Developers

Kristina Chodorow

O'REILLY®

Beijing · Cambridge · Farnham · Köln · Sebastopol · Tokyo

50 Tips and Tricks for MongoDB Developers
by Kristina Chodorow

Published by O'Reilly Media, Inc., 1005 Gravenstein Highway North, Sebastopol, CA 95472.

O'Reilly books may be purchased for educational, business, or sales promotional use. Online editions are also available for most titles (*http://my.safaribooksonline.com*). For more information, contact our corporate/institutional sales department: (800) 998-9938 or *corporate@oreilly.com*.

Editor: Mike Loukides	**Cover Designer:** Karen Montgomery
Proofreader: O'Reilly Production Services	**Interior Designer:** David Futato
	Illustrator: Robert Romano

Printing History:

April 2011:   First Edition.

ISBN: 978-1-449-30461-4

[LSI]

1302811504

Table of Contents

Preface

Getting started with MongoDB is easy, but once you're building applications with it more complex questions emerge. Is it better to store data using this schema or that one? Should I break this into two documents or store it all as one? How can I make this faster? The advice in this book should help you answer these questions.

This book is basically a list of tips, divided into topical sections:

Chapter 1, *Application Design Tips*
> Ideas to keep in mind when you design your schema.

Chapter 2, *Implementation Tips*
> Advice for programming applications against MongoDB.

Chapter 3, *Optimization Tips*
> Ways to speed up your application.

Chapter 4, *Data Safety and Consistency*
> How to use replication and journaling to keep data safe—without sacrificing too much performance.

Chapter 5, *Administration Tips*
> Advice for configuring MongoDB and keeping it running smoothly.

There are many tips that fit into more than one chapter, especially those concerning performance. The optimization chapter mainly focuses on indexing, but speed crops up everywhere, from schema design to implementation to data safety.

Who This Book Is For

This book is for people who are using MongoDB and know the basics. If you are not familiar with MongoDB, check out *MongoDB: The Definitive Guide* (*http://oreilly.com/catalog/0636920001096/*) (O'Reilly) or the MongoDB online documentation (*http://www.mongodb.org*).

Conventions Used in This Book

The following typographical conventions are used in this book:

Italic
> Indicates new terms, URLs, email addresses, filenames, and file extensions.

`Constant width`
> Used for program listings, as well as within paragraphs to refer to program elements such as variable or function names, databases, data types, environment variables, statements, and keywords.

`Constant width bold`
> Shows commands or other text that should be typed literally by the user.

`Constant width italic`
> Shows text that should be replaced with user-supplied values or by values determined by context.

 This icon signifies a tip, suggestion, or general note.

 This icon indicates a warning or caution.

Using Code Examples

This book is here to help you get your job done. In general, you may use the code in this book in your programs and documentation. You do not need to contact us for permission unless you're reproducing a significant portion of the code. For example, writing a program that uses several chunks of code from this book does not require permission. Selling or distributing a CD-ROM of examples from O'Reilly books does require permission. Answering a question by citing this book and quoting example code does not require permission. Incorporating a significant amount of example code from this book into your product's documentation does require permission.

We appreciate, but do not require, attribution. An attribution usually includes the title, author, publisher, and ISBN. For example: "*50 Tips and Tricks for MongoDB Developers* by Kristina Chodorow (O'Reilly). Copyright 2011 Kristina Chodorow, 978-1-449-30461-4."

If you feel your use of code examples falls outside fair use or the permission given above, feel free to contact us at *permissions@oreilly.com*.

Safari® Books Online

Safari Books Online is an on-demand digital library that lets you easily search over 7,500 technology and creative reference books and videos to find the answers you need quickly.

With a subscription, you can read any page and watch any video from our library online. Read books on your cell phone and mobile devices. Access new titles before they are available for print, and get exclusive access to manuscripts in development and post feedback for the authors. Copy and paste code samples, organize your favorites, download chapters, bookmark key sections, create notes, print out pages, and benefit from tons of other time-saving features.

O'Reilly Media has uploaded this book to the Safari Books Online service. To have full digital access to this book and others on similar topics from O'Reilly and other publishers, sign up for free at *http://my.safaribooksonline.com*.

How to Contact Us

Please address comments and questions concerning this book to the publisher:

O'Reilly Media, Inc.
1005 Gravenstein Highway North
Sebastopol, CA 95472
800-998-9938 (in the United States or Canada)
707-829-0515 (international or local)
707-829-0104 (fax)

We have a web page for this book, where we list errata, examples, and any additional information. You can access this page at:

http://www.oreilly.com/catalog/9781449304614

To comment or ask technical questions about this book, send email to:

bookquestions@oreilly.com

For more information about our books, courses, conferences, and news, see our website at *http://www.oreilly.com*.

Find us on Facebook: *http://facebook.com/oreilly*

Follow us on Twitter: *http://twitter.com/oreillymedia*

Watch us on YouTube: *http://www.youtube.com/oreillymedia*

CHAPTER 1

Application Design Tips

Tip #1: Duplicate data for speed, reference data for integrity

Data used by multiple documents can either be embedded (*denormalized*) or referenced (*normalized*). Denormalization isn't better than normalization and visa versa: each have their own trade-offs and you should choose to do whatever will work best with your application.

Denormalization can lead to inconsistent data: suppose you want to change the apple to a pear in Figure 1-1. If you change the value in one document but the application crashes before you can update the other documents, your database will have two different values for `fruit` floating around.

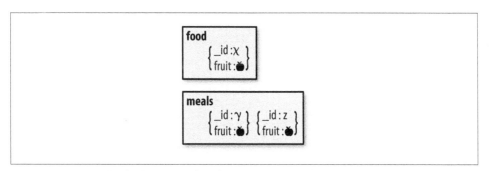

Figure 1-1. A normalized schema. The fruit field is stored in the food collection and referenced by the documents in the meals collection.

Inconsistency isn't great, but the level of "not-greatness" depends on what you're storing. For many applications, brief periods of inconsistency are OK: if someone changes his username, it might not matter that old posts show up with his old username for a few hours. If it's not OK to have inconsistent values even briefly, you should go with normalization.

However, if you normalize, your application must do an extra query every time it wants to find out what `fruit` is (Figure 1-2). If your application cannot afford this performance hit and it will be OK to reconcile inconsistencies later, you should denormalize.

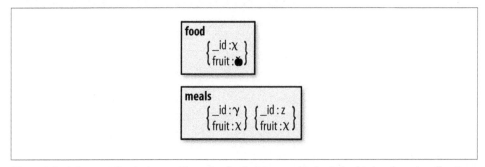

Figure 1-2. A denormalized schema. The value for fruit is stored in both the food and meals collections.

This is a trade-off: *you cannot have both the fastest performance and guaranteed immediate consistency.* You must decide which is more important for your application.

Example: a shopping cart order

Suppose that we are designing a schema for a shopping cart application. Our application stores orders in MongoDB, but what information should an order contain?

Normalized schema

A product:

```
{
    "_id" : productId,
    "name" : name,
    "price" : price,
    "desc" : description
}
```

An order:

```
{
    "_id" : orderId,
    "user" : userInfo,
    "items" : [
        productId1,
        productId2,
        productId3
    ]
}
```

We store the `_id` of each item in the order document. Then, when we display the contents of an order, we query the *orders* collection to get the correct order and then query the *products* collection to get the products associated with our list of `_ids`. *There is no way to get a the full order in a single query with this schema.*

If the information about a product is updated, all of the documents referencing this product will "change," as these documents merely point to the definitive document.

Normalization gives us slower reads and a consistent view across all orders; multiple documents can atomically change (as only the reference document is actually changing).

Denormalized schema

A product (same as previous):

```
{
    "_id" : productId,
    "name" : name,
    "price" : price,
    "desc" : description
}
```

An order:

```
{
    "_id" : orderId,
    "user" : userInfo,
    "items" : [
        {
            "_id" : productId1,
            "name" : name1,
            "price" : price1
        },
        {
            "_id" : productId2,
            "name" : name2,
            "price" : price2
        },
        {
            "_id" : productId3,
            "name" : name3,
            "price" : price3
        }
    ]
}
```

We store the product information as an embedded document in the order. Then, when we display an order, we only need to do a single query.

If the information about a product is updated and we want the change to be propagated to the orders, we must update every cart separately.

Denormalization gives us faster reads and a less consistent view across all orders; product details cannot be changed atomically across multiple documents.

So, given these options, how do you decide whether to normalize or denormalize?

Decision factors

There are three major factors to consider:

- *Are you paying a price on every read for the very rare occurrence of data changing?* You might read a product 10,000 times for every one time its details change. Do you want to pay a penalty on each of 10,000 reads to make that one write a bit quicker or guaranteed consistent? Most applications are much more read-heavy than write-heavy: figure out what your proportion is.

  How often does the data you're thinking of referencing actually change? The less it changes, the stronger the argument for denormalization. It is almost never worth referencing seldom-changing data such as names, birth dates, stock symbols, and addresses.

- *How important is consistency?* If consistency is important, you should go with normalization. For example, suppose multiple documents need to atomically see a change. If we were designing a trading application where certain securities could only be traded at certain times, we'd want to instantly "lock" them all when they were untradable. Then we could use a single lock document as a reference for the relevant group of securities documents. This sort of thing might be better to do at an application level, though, as the application will need to know the rules for when to lock and unlock anyway.

  Another time consistency is important is for applications where inconsistencies are difficult to reconcile. In the orders example, we have a strict hierarchy: orders get their information from products, products never get their information from orders. If there were multiple "source" documents, it would be difficult to decide which should win.

  However, in this (somewhat contrived) order application, consistency could actually be detrimental. Suppose we want to put a product on sale at 20% off. We don't want to change any information in the existing orders, we just want to update the product description. So, in this case, we actually want a snapshot of what the data looked like at a point in time (see "Tip #5: Embed "point-in-time" data" on page 7).

- *Do reads need to be fast?* If reads need to be as fast as possible, you should denormalize. In this application, they don't, so this isn't really a factor. Real-time applications should usually denormalize as much as possible.

There is a good case for denormalizing the order document: information doesn't change much and even when it does, we don't want orders to reflect the changes. Normalization doesn't give us any particular advantage here.

In this case, the best choice is to denormalize the *orders* schema.

Further reading:

- Your Coffee Shop Doesn't Use Two-Phase Commit (*http://www.eaipatterns.com/ docs/IEEE_Software_Design_2PC.pdf*) gives an example of how real-world systems handle consistency and how that relates to database design.

Tip #2: Normalize if you need to future-proof data

Normalization "future-proofs" your data: you should be able to use normalized data for different applications that will query the data in different ways in the future.

This assumes that you have some data set that application after application, for years and years, will have to use. There are data sets like this, but most people's data is constantly evolving, and old data is either updated or drops by the wayside. Most people want their database performing as fast as possible on the queries they're doing now, and if they change those queries in the future, they'll optimize their database for the new queries.

Also, if an application is successful, its data set often becomes very application-specific. That isn't to say it couldn't be used for more that one application; often you'll at least want to do meta-analysis on it. But this is hardly the same as "future-proofing" it to stand up to whatever queries people want to run in 10 years.

Tip #3: Try to fetch data in a single query

 Throughout this section, *application unit* is used as a general term for some application work. If you have a web or mobile application, you can think of an application unit as a request to the backend. Some other examples:

- For a desktop application, this might be a user interaction.
- For an analytics system, this might be one graph loaded.

It is basically a discrete unit of work that your application does that may involve accessing the database.

MongoDB schemas should be designed to do query per application unit.

Example: a blog

If we were designing a blog application, a request for a blog post might be one application unit. When we display a post, we want the content, tags, some information about the author (although probably not her whole profile), and the post's comments. Thus, we would embed all of this information in the post document and we could fetch everything needed for that view in one query.

Keep in mind that the goal is one query, not one document, per page: sometimes we might return multiple documents or portions of documents (not every field). For example, the main page might have the latest ten posts from the *posts* collection, but only their title, author, and a summary:

```
> db.posts.find({}, {"title" : 1, "author" : 1, "slug" : 1, "_id" : 0}).sort(
... {"date" : -1}).limit(10)
```

There might be a page for each tag that would have a list of the last 20 posts with the given tag:

```
> db.posts.find({"tag" : someTag}, {"title" : 1, "author" : 1,
... "slug" : 1, "_id" : 0}).sort({"date" : -1}).limit(20)
```

There would be a separate *authors* collection which would contain a complete profile for each author. An author page is simple, it would just be a document from the *authors* collection:

```
> db.authors.findOne({"name" : authorName})
```

Documents in the *posts* collection might contain a subset of the information that appears in the author document: maybe the author's name and thumbnail profile picture.

Note that an application unit does not have to correspond with a single document, although it happens to in some of the previously described cases (a blog post and an author's page are each contained in a single document). However, there are plenty of cases in which an application unit would be multiple documents, but accessible through a single query.

Example: an image board

Suppose we have an image board where users post messages consisting of an image and some text in either a new or an existing thread. Then an application unit is viewing 20 messages on a thread, so we'll have each person's post be a separate document in the *posts* collection. When we want to display a page, we'll do the query:

```
> db.posts.find({"threadId" : id}).sort({"date" : 1}).limit(20)
```

Then, when we want to get the next page of messages, we'll query for the next 20 messages on that thread, then the 20 after that, etc.:

```
> db.posts.find({"threadId" : id, "date" : {"$gt" : latestDateSeen}}).sort(
... {"date" : 1}).limit(20)
```

Then we could put an index on {threadId : 1, date : 1} to get good performance on these queries.

 We don't use skip(20), as ranges work better for pagination (*http://www .mongodb.org/display/DOCS/Advanced+Queries#AdvancedQueries -{{skip%28%29}}*).

As your application becomes more complicated and users and managers request more features, do not despair if you need to make more than one query per application unit. The one-query-per-unit goal is a good starting point and metric to judging your initial schema, but the real world is messy. With any sufficiently complex application, you're probably going to end up making more than one query for one of your application's more ridiculous features.

Tip #4: Embed dependent fields

When considering whether to embed or reference a document, ask yourself if you'll be querying for the information in this field by itself, or only in the framework of the larger document. For example, you might want to query on a tag, but only to link back to the posts with that tag, not for the tag on its own. Similarly with comments, you might have a list of recent comments, but people are interested in going to the post that inspired the comment (unless comments are first-class citizens in your application).

If you have been using a relational database and are migrating an existing schema to MongoDB, join tables are excellent candidates for embedding. Tables that are basically a key and a value—such as tags, permissions, or addresses—almost always work better embedded in MongoDB.

Finally, if only one document cares about certain information, embed the information in that document.

Tip #5: Embed "point-in-time" data

As mentioned in the orders example in "Tip #1: Duplicate data for speed, reference data for integrity" on page 1, you don't actually want the information in the order to change if a product, say, goes on sale or gets a new thumbnail. Any sort of information like this, where you want to snapshot the data at a particular time, should be embedded.

Another example from the order document: the address fields also fall into the "point-in-time" category of data. You don't want a user's past orders to change if he updates his profile.

Tip #6: Do not embed fields that have unbound growth

Because of the way MongoDB stores data, it is fairly inefficient to constantly be appending information to the end of an array. You want arrays and objects to be fairly constant in size during normal usage.

Thus, it is fine to embed 20 subdocuments, or 100, or 1,000,000, but do so up front. Allowing a document to grow a lot as it is used is probably going to be slower than you'd like.

Comments are often a weird edge case that varies on the application. Comments should, for most applications, be stored embedded in their parent document. However, for applications where the comments are their own entity or there are often hundreds or more, they should be stored as separate documents.

As another example, suppose we are creating an application solely for the purpose of commenting. The image board example in "Tip #3: Try to fetch data in a single query" on page 5 is like this; the primary content is the comments. In this case, we'd want comments to be separate documents.

Tip #7: Pre-populate anything you can

If you know that your document is going to need certain fields in the future, it is more efficient to populate them when you first insert it than to create the fields as you go. For example, suppose you are creating an application for site analytics, to see how many users visited different pages every minute over a day. We will have a pages collection, where each document represents a 6-hour slice in time for a page. We want to store info per minute and per hour:

```
{
    "_id" : pageId,
    "start" : time,
    "visits" : {
        "minutes" : [
            [num0, num1, ..., num59],
            [num0, num1, ..., num59],
            [num0, num1, ..., num59],
            [num0, num1, ..., num59],
            [num0, num1, ..., num59],
            [num0, num1, ..., num59]
        ],
        "hours" : [num0, ..., num5]
    }
}
```

We have a huge advantage here: we know what these documents are going to look like from now until the end of time. There will be one with a start time of now with an entry every minute for the next six hours. Then there will be another document like this, and another one.

Thus, we could have a batch job that either inserts these "template" documents at a non-busy time or in a steady trickle over the course of the day. This script could insert documents that look like this, replacing *someTime* with whatever the next 6-hour interval should be:

```
{
    "_id" : pageId,
    "start" : someTime,
    "visits" : {
        "minutes" : [
```

```
            [0, 0, ..., 0],
            [0, 0, ..., 0],
            [0, 0, ..., 0],
            [0, 0, ..., 0],
            [0, 0, ..., 0],
            [0, 0, ..., 0]
        ],
        "hours" : [0, 0, 0, 0, 0, 0]
    }
}
```

Now, when you increment or set these counters, MongoDB does not need to find space for them. It merely updates the values you've already entered, which is much faster.

For example, at the beginning of the hour, your program might do something like:

```
> db.pages.update({"_id" : pageId, "start" : thisHour},
... {"$inc" : {"visits.0.0" : 3}})
```

This idea can be extended to other types of data and even collections and databases themselves. If you use a new collection each day, you might as well create them in advance.

Tip #8: Preallocate space, whenever possible

This is closely related to both "Tip #6: Do not embed fields that have unbound growth" on page 7 and "Tip #7: Pre-populate anything you can" on page 8. This is an optimization for once you know that your documents usually grow to a certain size, but they start out at a smaller size. When you initially insert the document, add a garbage field that contains a string the size that the document will (eventually) be, then immediately unset that field:

```
> collection.insert({"_id" : 123, /* other fields */, "garbage" : someLongString})
> collection.update({"_id" : 123}, {"$unset" : {"garbage" : 1}})
```

This way, MongoDB will initially place the document somewhere that gives it enough room to grow (Figure 1-3).

Tip #9: Store embedded information in arrays for anonymous access

A question that often comes up is whether to embed information in an array or a sub-document. Subdocuments should be used when you'll always know exactly what you'll be querying for. If there is any chance that you won't know exactly what you're querying for, use an array. Arrays should usually be used when you know some criteria about the element you're querying for.

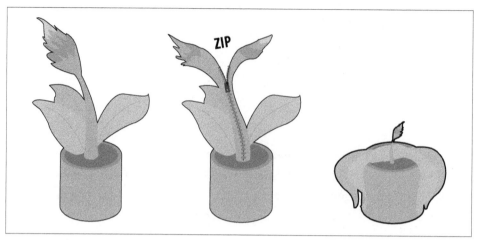

Figure 1-3. If you store a document with the amount of room it will need in the future, it will not need to be moved later.

Suppose we are programming a game where the player picks up various items. We might model the player document as:

```
{
    "_id" : "fred",
    "items" : {
        "slingshot" : {
            "type" : "weapon",
            "damage" : 23,
            "ranged" : true
        },
        "jar" : {
            "type" : "container",
            "contains" : "fairy"
        },
        "sword" : {
            "type" : "weapon",
            "damage" : 50,
            "ranged" : false
        }
    }
}
```

Now, suppose we want to find all weapons where damage is greater than 20. We can't! Subdocuments do not allow you to reach into `items` and say, "Give me any item with damage greater than 20." You can only ask for *specific* items: "Is `items.slingshot.dam age` greater than 20? How about `items.sword.damage`?" and so on.

If you want to be able to access any item without knowing its identifier, you should arrange your schema to store items in an array:

```
{
    "_id" : "fred",
```

```
"items" : [
    {
        "id" : "slingshot",
        "type" : "weapon",
        "damage" : 23,
        "ranged" : true
    },
    {

        "id" : "jar",
        "type" : "container",
        "contains" : "fairy"
    },
    {

        "id" : "sword",
        "type" : "weapon",
        "damage" : 50,
        "ranged" : false
    }
    ]
}
```

Now you can use a simple query such as {"items.damage" : {"$gt" : 20}}. If you need more than one criteria of a given item matched (say, damage and ranged), you can use $elemMatch (*http://www.mongodb.org/display/DOCS/Advanced+Queries#AdvancedQueries-%24elemMatch*).

So, when should you use a subdocument instead of an array? When you know and will always know the name of the field that you are accessing.

For example, suppose we keep track of a player's abilities: her strength, intelligence, wisdom, dexterity, constitution, and charisma. We will always know which specific ability we are looking for, so we could store this as:

```
{
    "_id" : "fred",
    "race" : "gnome",
    "class" : "illusionist",
    "abilities" : {
        "str" : 20,
        "int" : 12,
        "wis" : 18,
        "dex" : 24,
        "con" : 23,
        "cha" : 22
    }
}
```

When we want to find a specific skill, we can look up abilities.str, or abilities.con, or whatever. We'll never want to find some ability that's greater than 20, we'll always know what we're looking for.

Tip #10: Design documents to be self-sufficient

MongoDB is supposed to be a big, dumb data store. That is, it does almost no processing, it just stores and retrieves data. You should respect this goal and try to avoid forcing MongoDB to do any computation that could be done on the client. Even "trivial" tasks, such finding averages or summing fields should generally be pushed to the client.

If you want to query for information that must be computed and is not explicitly present in your document, you have two choices:

- Incur a serious performance penalty (forcing MongoDB to do the computation using JavaScript, see "Tip #11: Prefer $-operators to JavaScript" on page 13)
- Make the information explicit in your document

Generally, you should just make the information explicit in your document.

Suppose you want to query for documents where the total number of apples and oranges is 30. That is, your documents look something like:

```
{
    "_id" : 123,
    "apples" : 10,
    "oranges" : 5
}
```

Querying for the total, given the document above, will require JavaScript and thus is very inefficient. Instead, add a total field to the document:

```
{
    "_id" : 123,
    "apples" : 10,
    "oranges" : 5,
    "total" : 15
}
```

Then this total field can be incremented when apples or oranges are changed:

```
> db.food.update(criteria,
... {"$inc" : {"apples" : 10, "oranges" : -2, "total" : 8}})
> db.food.findOne()
{
    "_id" : 123,
    "apples" : 20,
    "oranges" : 3,
    "total" : 23
}
```

This becomes trickier if you aren't sure whether an update will change anything. For example, suppose you want to be able to query for the number types of fruit, but you don't know whether your update will add a new type.

So, suppose your documents looked something like this:

```
{
    "_id" : 123,
    "apples" : 20,
    "oranges : 3,
    "total" : 2
}
```

Now, if you do an update that might or might not create a new field, do you increment total or not? If the update ends up creating a new field, total should be updated:

```
> db.food.update({"_id" : 123}, {"$inc" : {"banana" : 3, "total" : 1}})
```

Conversely, if the banana field already exists, we shouldn't increment the total. But from the client side, we don't know whether it exists!

There are two ways of dealing with this that are probably becoming familiar: the fast, inconsistent way, and the slow, consistent way.

The fast way is to chose to either add or not add 1 to total and make our application aware that it'll need to check the actual total on the client side. We can have an ongoing batch job that corrects any inconsistencies we end up with.

If our application can take the extra time immediately, we could do a findAndModify that "locks" the document (setting a "locked" field that other writes will manually check), return the document, and then issue an update unlocking the document and updating the fields and total correctly:

```
> var result = db.runCommand({"findAndModify" : "food",
... "query" : {/* other criteria */, "locked" : false},
... "update" : {"$set" : {"locked" : true}}})
>
> if ("banana" in result.value) {
...     db.fruit.update(criteria, {"$set" : {"locked" : false},
...         "$inc" : {"banana" : 3}})
... } else {
...     // increment total if banana field doesn't exist yet
...     db.fruit.update(criteria, {"$set" : {"locked" : false},
...         "$inc" : {"banana" : 3, "total" : 1}})
... }
```

The correct choice depends on your application.

Tip #11: Prefer $-operators to JavaScript

Certain operations cannot be done with $-operators. For most applications, making a document self-sufficient will minimize the complexity of the queries that you must do. However, sometimes you will have to query for something that you cannot express with $-operators. In that case, JavaScript can come to your rescue: you can use a $where clause to execute arbitrary JavaScript as part of your query.

To use `$where` in a query, write a JavaScript function that returns `true` or `false` (whether that document matches the `$where` or not). So, suppose we only wanted to return records where the value of `member[0].age` and `member[1].age` are equal. We could do this with:

```
> db.members.find({"$where" : function() {
... return this.member[0].age == this.member[1].age;
... }})
```

As you might imagine, `$where` gives your queries quite a lot of power. However, it is also slow.

Behind the scenes

`$where` takes a long time because of what MongoDB is doing behind the scenes: when you perform a normal (non-`$where`) query, your client turns that query into BSON (*http://www.bsonspec.org*) and sends it to the database. MongoDB stores data in BSON, too, so it can basically compare your query directly against the data. This is very fast and efficient.

Now suppose you have a `$where` clause that must be executed as part of your query. MongoDB will have to create a JavaScript object for every document in the collection, parsing the documents' BSON and adding all of their fields to the JavaScript objects. Then it executes the JavaScript you sent against the documents, then tears it all down again. This is extremely time- and resource-intensive.

Getting better performance

`$where` is a good hack when necessary, but it should be avoided whenever possible. In fact, if you notice that your queries require lots of `$where`s, that is a good indication that you should rethink your schema.

If a `$where` query is needed, you can cut down on the performance hit by minimizing the number of documents that make it to the `$where`. Try to come up with other criteria that can be checked without a `$where` and list that criteria first; the fewer documents that are "in the running" by the time the query gets to the `$where`, the less time the `$where` will take.

For example, suppose that we have the `$where` example given above, and we realize that, as we're checking two members' ages, we are only for members with at least a joint membership, maybe a family members:

```
> db.members.find({'type' : {$in : ['joint', 'family']},
... "$where" : function() {
...        return this.member[0].age == this.member[1].age;
... }})
```

Now all single membership documents will be excluded by the time the query gets to the `$where`.

Tip #12: Compute aggregations as you go

Whenever possible, compute aggregations over time with $inc. For example, in "Tip #7: Pre-populate anything you can" on page 8, we have an analytics application with stats by the minute and the hour. We can increment the hour stats at the same time that we increment the minute ones.

If your aggregations need more munging (for example, finding the average number of queries over the hour), store the data in the minutes field and then have an ongoing batch process that computes averages from the latest minutes. As all of the information necessary to compute the aggregation is stored in one document, this processing could even be passed off to the client for newer (unaggregated) documents. Older documents would have already been tallied by the batch job.

Tip #13: Write code to handle data integrity issues

Given MongoDB's schemaless nature and the advantages to denormalizing, you'll need to keep your data consistent in your application.

Many ODMs have ways of enforcing consistent schemas to various levels of strictness. However, there are also the consistency issues brought up above: data inconsistencies caused by system failures ("Tip #1: Duplicate data for speed, reference data for integrity" on page 1) and limitations of MongoDB's updates ("Tip #10: Design documents to be self-sufficient" on page 12). For these types of inconsistencies, you'll need to actually write a script that will check your data.

If you follow the tips in this chapter, you might end up with quite a few cron jobs, depending on your application. For example, you might have:

Consistency fixer
> Check computations and duplicate data to make sure that everyone has consistent values.

Pre-populator
> Create documents that will be needed in the future.

Aggregator
> Keep inline aggregations up-to-date.

Other useful scripts (not strictly related to this chapter) might be:

Schema checker
> Make sure the set of documents currently being used all have a certain set of fields, either correcting them automatically or notifying you about incorrect ones.

Backup job
> fsync, lock, and dump your database at regular intervals.

Running jobs in the background that check and protect your data give you more lassitude to play with it.

CHAPTER 2

Implementation Tips

Tip #14: Use the correct types

Storing data using the correct types will make your life easier. Data type affects how data can be queried, the order in which MongoDB will sort it, and how many bytes of storage it takes up.

Numbers

Any field you'll be using as a number should be saved as a number. This means if you wish to increment the value or sort it in numeric order. However, what kind of number? Well, often it doesn't matter—sometimes it does.

Sorting compares all numeric types equally: if you had a 32-bit integer, a 64-bit integer, and a double with values 2, 1, and 1.5, they would end up sorted in the correct order. However, certain operations demand certain types: bit operations (AND and OR) only work on integer fields (not doubles).

The database will automatically turn 32-bit integers into 64-bit integers if they are going to overflow (due to an $inc, say), so you don't have to worry about that.

Dates

Similarly to numbers, exact dates should be saved using the date type. However, dates such as birthdays are not exact; who knows their birth time down to the millisecond? For dates such as these, it often works just as well to use ISO-format dates: a string of the form *yyyy-mm-dd*. This will sort birthdays correctly and match them more flexibly than if you used dates, which force you to match birthdays to the millisecond.

Strings

All strings in MongoDB must be UTF-8 encoded, so strings in other encodings must be either converted to UTF-8 or saved as binary data.

ObjectIds

Always save ObjectIds as ObjectIds, not as strings. This is important for several reasons. First, queryability: strings do not match ObjectIds and ObjectIds do not match strings. Second, ObjectIds are useful: most drivers have methods that can automatically extract the date a document was created from its `ObjectId`. Finally, the string representation of an `ObjectId` is more than twice the size, on disk, as an `ObjectId`.

Tip #15: Override _id when you have your own simple, unique id

If your data doesn't have a naturally occurring unique field (often the case), go ahead and use the default `ObjectId` for `_id`s. However, if your data does have a unique field and you don't need the properties of an `ObjectId`, then go ahead and override the default `_id`—use your own unique value. This saves a bit of space and is particularly useful if you were going to index your unique id, as this will save you an entire index in space and resources (a very significant savings).

There are a couple reasons *not* to use your own `_id` that you should consider: first, you must be very confident that it is unique or be willing to handle duplicate key exceptions. Second, you should keep in mind the tree structure of an index (see "Tip #22: Use indexes to do more with less memory" on page 24) and how random or non-random your insertion order will be. `ObjectId`s have an excellent insertion order as far as the index tree is concerned: they always are increasing, meaning they are always being inserted at the right edge of the B-tree. This, in turn, means that MongoDB only has to keep the right edge of the B-tree in memory.

Conversely, a random value in the `_id` field means that `_id`s will be inserted all over the tree. Then the machine must move a page of the index into memory, update a tiny piece of it, then probably ignore it until it slides out of memory again. This is less efficient.

Tip #16: Avoid using a document for _id

You should almost never use a document as your `_id` value, although it may be un-avoidable in certain situations (such as the output of a MapReduce). The problem with using a document as `_id` is that *indexing a document* is very different than *indexing the fields within a document*. So, if you aren't planning to query for the whole subdocument every time, you may end up with multiple indexes on `_id`, `_id.foo`, `_id.bar`, etc., any-way.

You also cannot change `_id` without overwriting the entire document, so it's impractical to use it if fields of the subdocument might change.

Tip #17: Do not use database references

 This tip is specifically about the special *database reference* subdocument type, not references (as discussed in the previous chapter) in general.

Database references are normal subdocuments of the form {$id : *identifier*, $ref : *collectionName*} (they can, optionally, also have a $db field for the database name). They feel a bit relational: you're sort of referencing a document in another collection. However, you're not really referencing another collection, this is *just a normal subdocument*. It does absolutely nothing magical. MongoDB cannot dereference database references on the fly; they are not a way of doing joins in MongoDB. They are just subdocuments holding an _id and collection name. This means that, in order to dereference them, you must query the database a second time.

If you are referencing a document but already know the collection, you might as well save the space and store just the _id, not the _id and the collection name. A database reference is a waste of space unless you do not know what collection the referenced document will be in.

The only time I've heard of a database reference being used to good effect was for a system that allowed users to comment on anything in the system. They had a *comments* collection, and stored comments in that with references to nearly every other collection and database in the system.

Tip #18: Don't use GridFS for small binary data

GridFS requires two queries: one to fetch a file's metadata and one to fetch its contents (Figure 2-1). Thus, if you use GridFS to store small files, you are doubling the number of queries that your application has to do. GridFS is basically a way of breaking up large binary objects for storage in the database.

GridFS is for storing big data—larger than will fit in a single document. As a rule of thumb, anything that is too big to load all at once on the client is probably not something you want to load all at once on the server. Therefore, anything you're going to stream to a client is a good candidate for GridFS. Things that will be loaded all at once on the client, such as images, sounds, or even small video clips, should generally just be embedded in your main document.

Further reading:

- How GridFS works (*http://www.mongodb.org/display/DOCS/GridFS*)

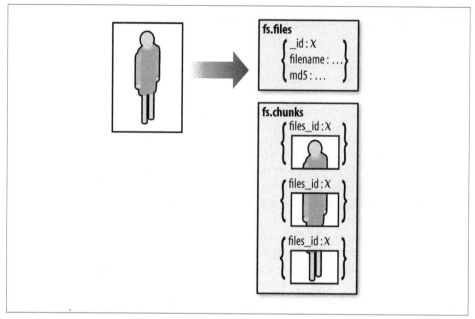

Figure 2-1. GridFS breaks up large pieces of data and stores them in chunks.

Tip #19: Handle "seamless" failover

Often people have heard that MongoDB handles failover seamlessly and are surprised when they start getting exceptions. MongoDB tries to recover from failures without intervention, but handling certain errors is impossible for it to do automatically.

Suppose that you send a request to the server and you get back a network error. Now your driver has a couple options.

If the driver can't reconnect to the database, then it obviously can't automatically retry sending the request to that server. However, suppose you have another server that the driver knows about, could it automatically send the request to that one? Well, it depends on what the request was. If you were going to send a write to the primary, probably there is no other primary yet. If you were going to do a read, it could be something like a long-running MapReduce to a slave that's now down, and the driver shouldn't send that to some other random server (the primary?). So, it can't auto-retry to a different server.

If the error was a temporary network blip and the driver reconnects to the server immediately, it still shouldn't try to send the request again. What if the driver sent the original message and then encountered a network error, or errored out on the database response? Then the request might already be being processed by the database, so you wouldn't want to send it a second time.

This is a tricky problem that is often application-dependent, so the drivers punt on the issue. You must catch whatever exception is thrown on network errors (you should be able to find info about how to do this in your driver's documentation). Handle the exception and then figure out on a request-by-request basis: do you want to resend the message? Do you need to check state on the database first? Can you just give up, or do you need to keep retrying?

Tip #20: Handle replica set failure and failover

Your application should be able to handle all of the exciting failure scenarios that could occur with a replica set.

Suppose your application throws a "not master" error. There are a couple possible causes for this error: your set might be failing over to a new primary and you have to handle the time during the primary's election gracefully. The time it takes for an election varies: it's usually a few seconds, but if you're unlucky it could be 30 seconds or more. If you're on the wrong side of a network partition, you might not be able to see a master for hours.

Not being able to see a master at all is an important case to handle: can your application drop into read-only mode if this happens? Your application should be able to handle being read-only for short periods (during a master election) and long periods (when a majority is down or partitioned).

Regardless of whether there's a master, you should be able to continue sending reads to whichever members of the set you can reach.

Members may briefly go through an unreadable "recovering" phase during elections: members in this state will throw errors about not being masters or secondaries if your driver tries to read from them, and may be in this state so fleetingly that these errors slip in between the pings drivers send to the database.

CHAPTER 3

Optimization Tips

When you're programming an application, you generally want the database to respond instantly to anything you do. To maximize its ability to do this, it's important to know what takes up time.

Tip #21: Minimize disk access

Accessing data from RAM is fast and accessing data from disk is slow. Therefore, most optimization techniques are basically fancy ways of minimizing the amount of disk accesses.

Fuzzy Math

Reading from disk is (about) a million times slower than reading from memory.

Most spinning disk drives can access data in, say, 10 milliseconds, whereas memory returns data in 10 nanoseconds. (This depends a lot on what kind of hard drive you have and what kind of RAM you have, but we'll do a very broad generalization that is roughly accurate for most people.) This means that the ratio of disk time to RAM time is 1 millisecond to 1 nanosecond. One millisecond is equal to one million nanoseconds, so accessing disk takes (roughly) a million times longer than accessing RAM.

Thus, reading off of disk takes a *really* long time in computing terms.

 On Linux, you can measure sequential disk access on your machine by running `sudo hdparm -t /dev/hdwhatever`. This doesn't give you an exact measure, as MongoDB will be doing non-sequential reads and writes, but it's interesting to see what your machine can do.

So, what can be done about this? There are a couple "easy" solutions:

Use SSDs

> SSDs (solid state drives) are much faster than spinning hard disks for many things, but they are often smaller, more expensive, are difficult to securely erase, and still do not come close to the speed at which you can read from memory. This isn't to discourage you from using them: they usually work fantastically with MongoDB, but they aren't a magical cure-all.

Add more RAM

> Adding more RAM means you have to hit disk less. However, adding RAM will only get you so far—at some point, your data isn't going to fit in RAM anymore.

So, the question becomes: how do we store terabytes (petabytes?) of data on disk, but program an application that will mostly access data already in memory *and* move data from disk to memory as infrequently as possible?

If you literally access all of your data randomly in real time, you're just going to need a lot of RAM. However, most applications don't: recent data is accessed more than older data, certain users are more active than others, certain regions have more customers than others. Applications like these can be designed to keep certain documents in memory and go to disk very infrequently.

Tip #22: Use indexes to do more with less memory

First, just so we're all on the same page, Figure 3-1 shows the sequence a read request takes.

We'll assume, for this book, that a page of memory is 4KB, although this is not universally true.

So, let's say you have a machine with 256GB of data and 16GB of memory. Let's say most of this data is in one collection and you query this collection. What does MongoDB do?

MongoDB loads the first page of documents from disk into memory, and compares those to your query. Then it loads the next page and compares those. Then it loads the next page. And so on, through 256GB of data. It can't take any shortcuts: it cannot know if a document matches without looking at the document, so it must look at every document. Thus, it will need to load all 256GB into memory (the OS takes care of swapping the oldest pages out of memory as it needs room for new ones). This is going to take a long, long time.

How can we avoid loading all 256GB into memory every time we do a query? We can tell MongoDB to create an index on a given field, *x*, and MongoDB will create a tree of the collection's values for that field. MongoDB basically preprocesses the data, adding every *x* value in the collection to an ordered tree (see Figure 3-2). Each index entry in the tree contains a value of *x* and a pointer to the document with that *x* value. The tree

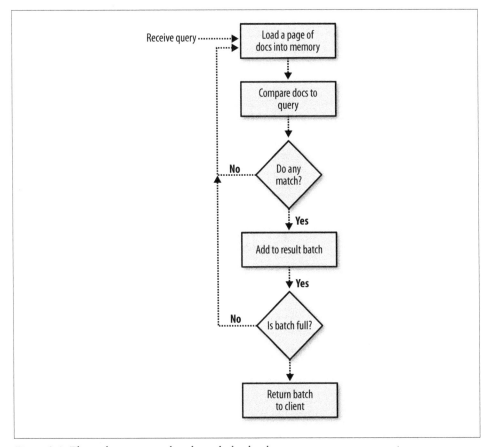

Figure 3-1. The path a request takes through the database.

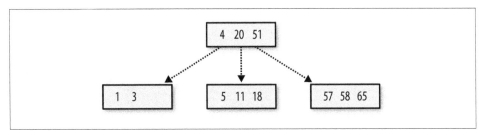

Figure 3-2. A B-tree, possibly for an index on a field with integer values.

just contains a pointer to the document, not the document itself, meaning the index is generally much smaller than the entire collection.

When your query includes *x* as part of the criteria, MongoDB will notice that it has an index on *x* and will look through the ordered tree of values. Now, instead of looking through every document, MongoDB can say, "Is the value I'm looking for greater than or less than this tree node's values? If greater, go to the right, if less, go to the left." It continues in this manner until it either finds the value it's looking for or it sees that the value it's looking for doesn't exist. If it finds the value, it then follows the pointer to the actual document, loading that document's page into memory and then returning it (Figure 3-3).

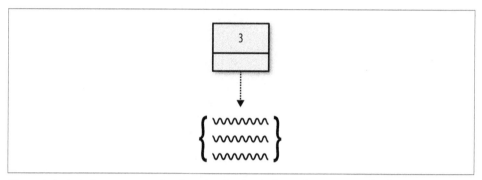

Figure 3-3. An index entry contains the value for that index and a pointer to the document.

So, suppose we do a query that will end up matching a document or two in our collection. If we do not use an index, we must load 64 million pages into memory from disk:

> Pages of data: 256GB / (4KB/page) = 64 million pages

Suppose our index is about 80GB in size. Then the index is about 20 million pages in size:

> Number of pages in our index: 80GB / (4KB/page) = 20 million pages

However, the index is ordered, meaning that we don't have to go through every entry: we only have to load certain nodes. How many?

> Number of pages of the index that must be loaded into memory: $ln(20,000,000)$ = 17 pages

From 64,000,000 down to 17!

OK, so it isn't exactly 17: once we've found the result in the index we need to load the document from memory, so that's another size-of-document pages loaded, plus nodes in the tree might be more than one page in size. Still, it's a tiny number of pages compared with traversing the entire collection!

Hopefully you can now picture how indexes helps queries go faster.

Tip #23: Don't always use an index

Now that I have you reeling with the usefulness of indexes, let me warn you that they should not be used for all queries. Suppose that, in the example above, instead of fetching a few records we were returning about 90% of the document in the collection.

If we use an index for this type of query, we'd end up looking through most of the index tree, loading, say, 60GB of the index into memory. Then we'd have to follow all of the pointers in the index, loading 230GB of data from the collection. We'd end up loading 230GB + 60GB = 290GB—more than if we hadn't used an index at all!

Thus, indexes are generally most useful when you have a small subset of the total data that you want returned. A good rule of thumb is that they stop being useful once you are returning approximately half of the data in a collection.

If you have an index on a field but you're doing a large query that would be less efficient using that index, you can force MongoDB not to use an index by sorting by {"$natural" : 1}. This sort means "return data in the order it appears on disk," which forces MongoDB to not use an index:

```
> db.foo.find().sort({"$natural" : 1})
```

If a query does not use an index, MongoDB does a *table scan*, which means it looks through all of the documents in the collection to find the results.

Write speed

Every time a new record is added, removed, or updated, every index affected by the change must be updated. Suppose you insert a document. For each index, MongoDB has to find where the new document's value falls on the index's tree and then insert it there. For deletes, it must find and remove an entry from the tree. For updates, it might add a new index entry like an insert, remove an entry like a delete, or have to do both if the value changes. Thus, indexes can add quite a lot of overhead to writes.

Tip #24: Create indexes that cover your queries

If we only want certain fields returned and can include all of these fields in the index, MongoDB can do a *covered index* query, where it never has to follow the pointers to documents and just returns the index's data to the client. So, for example, suppose we have an index on some set of fields:

```
> db.foo.ensureIndex({"x" : 1, "y" : 1, "z" : 1})
```

Then if we query on the indexed fields and only request the indexed fields returned, there's no reason for MongoDB to load the full document:

```
> db.foo.find({"x" : criteria, "y" : criteria},
... {"x" : 1, "y" : 1, "z" : 1, "_id" : 0})
```

Now this query will only touch the data in the index, it never has to touch the collection proper.

Notice that we include a clause "_id" : 0 in the fields-to-return argument. The _id is always returned, by default, but it's not part of our index so MongoDB would have to go to the document to fetch the `_id`. Removing it from the fields-to-return means that MongoDB can just return the values from the index.

If some queries only return a few fields, consider throwing these fields into your index so that you can do covered index queries, even if they aren't going to be searched on. For example, z is not used in the query above, but it is a field in the fields-to-return and, thus, the index.

Tip #25: Use compound indexes to make multiple queries fast

If possible, create a compound index that can be used by multiple queries. This isn't always possible, but if you do multiple queries with similar arguments, it may be.

Any query that matches the prefix of an index can use the index. Therefore, you want to create indexes with the greatest number of criteria shared between queries.

Suppose that your application runs these queries:

```
collection.find({"x" : criteria, "y" : criteria, "z" : criteria})
collection.find({"z" : criteria, "y" : criteria, "w" : criteria})
collection.find({"y" : criteria, "w" : criteria})
```

As you can see, y is the only field that appears in each query, so that's a very good candidate to go in the index. z appears in the first two, and w appears in the second two, so either of those would work as the next option (see more on index ordering in "Tip #27: AND-queries should match as little as possible as fast as possible" on page 30 and "Tip #28: OR-queries should match as much as possible as soon as possible" on page 31).

We want to hit this index as much and as often as possible. If a certain query above is more important than the others or will be run much more frequently, our index should favor that one. For example, suppose the first query is going to be run thousands of times more than the next two. Then we want to favor that one in our index:

```
collection.ensureIndex({"y" : 1, "z" : 1, "x" : 1})
```

The the first query will be as highly optimized as possible and the next two will use the index for part of the query.

If all three queries will be run approximately the same amount, a good index might be:

```
collection.ensureIndex({"y" : 1, "w" : 1, "z" : 1})
```

Then all three will be able to use the index for the y criteria, the second two will be able to use it for w, and the middle one will be able to fully use the index.

You can use explain to see how an index is being used on a query:

```
collection.find(criteria).explain()
```

Tip #26: Create hierarchical documents for faster scans

Keeping your data organized hierarchically not only keeps it organized, but MongoDB can also search it faster without an index (in some cases).

For example, suppose that you have a query that does not use an index. As mentioned previously, MongoDB has to look through every document in the collection to see if anything matches the query criteria. This can take a varying length of time, depending on how you structure your documents.

Let's say you have user documents with a flat structure like this:

```
{
    "_id" : id,
    "name" : username,
    "email" : email,
    "twitter" : username,
    "screenname" : username,
    "facebook" : username,
    "linkedin" : username,
    "phone" : number,
    "street" : street
    "city" : city,
    "state" : state,
    "zip" : zip,
    "fax" : number
}
```

Now suppose we query:

```
> db.users.find({"zip" : "10003"})
```

What does MongoDB do? It has to look through every field of every document, looking for the zip field (Figure 3-4).

Figure 3-4. MongoDB must look through each field in the document if there is no hierarchy.

By using embedded documents, we can create our own "tree" and let MongoDB do this faster. Suppose we change our schema to look like this:

```
{
    "_id" : id,
    "name" : username,
```

```
    "online" : {
        "email" : email,
        "twitter" : username,
        "screenname" : username,
        "facebook" : username,
        "linkedin" : username,
    },
    "address" : {
        "street" : street,
        "city" : city,
        "state" : state,
        "zip" : zip
    }
    "tele" : {
        "phone" : number,
        "fax" : number,
    }
}
```

Now our query would look like this:

```
> db.users.find({"address.zip" : "10003"})
```

And MongoDB would only have to look at _id, name, and online before seeing that address was a desired prefix and then looking for zip within that. Using a sensible hierarchy allows MongoDB not to inspect every field looking for a match.

Tip #27: AND-queries should match as little as possible as fast as possible

Suppose we are querying for documents matching criteria *A*, *B*, and *C*. Now, let's say that criteria *A* matches 40,000 documents, *B* matches 9,000, and *C* matches 200. If we query MongoDB with the criteria in the order given, it will not be very efficient (see Figure 3-5).

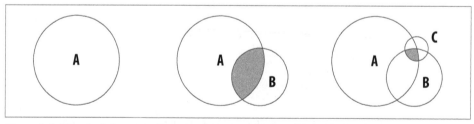

Figure 3-5. The shaded area is the space that must be queried at each step. Querying from largest result set to smallest result set means querying comparatively large numbers of documents.

If we put *C* first, then *B*, then *A*, we only have to look at 200 documents (at most) for the *B* and *C* criteria (Figure 3-6).

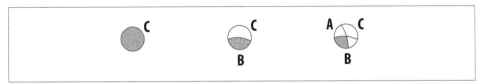

Figure 3-6. By querying for C first, we cut down the search space dramatically for later queries.

As you can see, this brings down the amount of work quite a bit. If you know that a certain criteria is going to match less documents, make sure that criteria goes first (especially if it is indexed).

Tip #28: OR-queries should match as much as possible as soon as possible

OR-style queries are exactly the opposite of AND queries: try to put the most inclusive clauses first, as MongoDB has to keep checking documents that aren't part of the result set yet for every match.

If we do it in the same order we were structuring the AND-query in, we have to check documents for each clause (Figure 3-7).

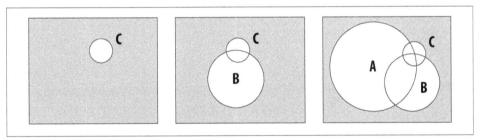

Figure 3-7. The rectangle is the collection, the shaded area is the parts of the collection that must be searched at each step. Searching for C first forces us to retry most of the space on each subsequent query.

Instead, we match as much of the collection as possible as soon as possible (Figure 3-8).

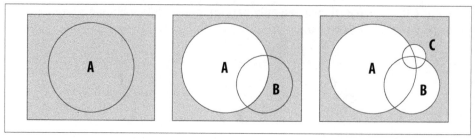

Figure 3-8. By querying for the largest result first, we limit the search space for subsequent queries.

CHAPTER 4

Data Safety and Consistency

Tip #29: Write to the journal for single server, replicas for multiserver

In an ideal world, all writes would be instantly, permanently saved to disks and be instantly retrievable from anywhere. Unfortunately, this is impossible in the real world, you can either take more time to make sure your data is safe or save it faster with less safety. MongoDB gives you more knobs to twiddle in this area than it has knobs for everything else combined and it's important to understand your options.

Replication and journaling are the two approaches to data safety that you can take with MongoDB.

Generally, you should run with replication and have at least one of your servers journaled. The MongoDB blog has a good post (*http://blog.mongodb.org/post/381927266/ what-about-durability*) on why you shouldn't run MongoDB (or any database) on a single server.

MongoDB's replication automatically copies all of your writes to other servers. If your current master goes down, you can bring up another server as the new master (this happens automatically with replica sets).

If a member of a replica set shuts down uncleanly and it was not running with -- journal, MongoDB makes no guarantees about its data (it may be corrupt). You have to get a clean copy of the data: either wipe the data and resync it or load a backup and fastsync (*http://www.mongodb.org/display/DOCS/Upgrading+to+Replica+Sets#Upgra dingtoReplicaSets-UsingaSlave%27sExistingData*).

Journaling gives you data safety on a single server. All operations are written to a log (the *journal*) that is flushed to disk regularly. If your machine crashes but the hardware is OK, you can restart the server and the data will repair itself by reading the journal. Keep in mind that MongoDB cannot save you from hardware problems: if your disk gets corrupted or damaged, your database will probably not be recoverable.

Replication and journaling can be used at the same time, but you must do this strategically to minimize the performance penalty. Both methods basically make a copy of all writes, so you have:

No safety
> One server write per write request

Replication
> Two server writes per write request

Journaling
> Two server writes per write request

Replication+journaling
> Three server writes per write request

Writing each piece of information three times is a lot, but if your application does not require high performance and data safety is very important, you could consider using both. There are some very safe alternative deployments that are more performant covered next.

Tip #30: Always use replication, journaling, or both

If you're running a single server, use the `--journal` option.

 In development, there is no reason not to use `--journal` all of the time. Add journaling to your local MongoDB configuration to make sure that you don't lose data while in development.

Given the performance penalties involved in using journaling, you might want to mix journaled an unjournaled servers if you have multiple machines. Backup slaves could be journaled, whereas primaries and secondaries (especially those balancing read load) could be unjournaled.

A sturdy small setup is shown in Figure 4-1. The primary and secondary are not run with journaling, keeping them fast for reads and writes. In a normal server crash, you can fail over to the secondary and restart the crashed machine at your leisure.

If either data center goes down entirely, you still have a safe copy of your data. If DC2 goes down, once it's up again you can restart the backup server. If DC1 goes down, you can either make the backup machine master, or use its data to re-seed the machines in DC1. If both data centers go down, you at least have a backup in DC2 that you can bootstrap everything from.

Another safe setup for five servers is shown in Figure 4-2. This is a slightly more robust setup than above: there are secondaries in both data centers, a delayed member to protect against user error, and a journaled member for backup.

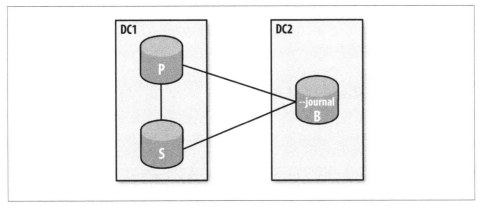

Figure 4-1. A primary (P), secondary (S), and backup server run with journaling (B).

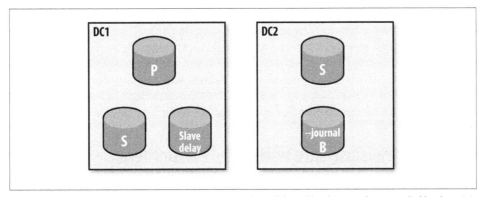

Figure 4-2. A primary (P), two secondaries (S), one slave-delayed backup, and a journaled backup (B).

Tip #31: Do not depend on repair to recover data

If your database crashes and you were not running with --journal, *do not use that server's data as-is*. It might seem fine for weeks until you suddenly access a corrupt document which causes your application to go screwy. Or your indexes might be messed up so you only get partial results back from the database. Or a hundred other things; corruption is bad, insidious, and often undetectable...for a while.

You have a couple of options. You can run repair (*http://www.mongodb.org/display/ DOCS/Durability+and+Repair#DurabilityandRepair-RepairCommand*). This is a tempting option, but it's really a last resort. First, repair goes through every document it can find and makes a clean copy of it. This takes a long time, a lot of disk space (an equal amount to the space currently being used), and skips any corrupted records. This means that if it can't find millions of documents because of corruption, it will not copy them and they will be lost. Your database may not be corrupted anymore, but it also may be much smaller. Also, repair doesn't introspect the documents: there could be corruption that makes certain fields unparsable that repair will not find or fix.

The preferable option is fastsyncing from a backup or resyncing from scratch. Remember that you must wipe the possibly corrupt data before resyncing; MongoDB's replication cannot "fix" corrupted data.

Tip #32: Understand getlasterror

By default, writes do not return any response from the database. If you send the database an update, insert, or remove, it will process it and not return anything to the user. Thus, drivers do not expect any response on either success or failure.

However, obviously there are a lot of situations where you'd like to have a response from the database. To handle this, MongoDB has an "about that last operation..." command, called getlasterror. Originally, it just described any errors that occurred in the last operation, but has branched out into giving all sorts of information about the write and providing a variety of safety-related options.

To avoid any inadvertent read-your-last-write mistakes (see "Tip #50: Use a single connection to read your own writes" on page 51), getlasterror is stuck to the butt of a write request, essentially forcing the database to treat the write and getlasterror as a single request. They are sent together and guaranteed to be processed one after the other, with no other operations in between. The drivers bundle this functionality in so you don't have to take care of it yourself, generally calling it a "safe" write.

Tip #33: Always use safe writes in development

In development, you want to make sure that your application is behaving as you expect and safe writes can help you with that. What sort of things could go wrong with a write? A write could try to push something onto a non-array field, cause a duplicate key exception (trying to store two documents with the same value in a uniquely indexed field), remove an _id field, or a million other user errors. You'll want to know that the write isn't valid before you deploy.

One insidious error is running out of disk space: all of a sudden queries are mysteriously returning less data. This one is tricky if you are not using safe writes, as free disk space isn't something that you usually check. I've often accidentally set --dbpath to the wrong partition, causing MongoDB to run out of space much sooner than planned.

During development, there are lots of reasons that a write might not go through due to developer error, and you'll want to know about them.

Tip #34: Use w with replication

For important operations, you should make sure that the writes have been replicated to a majority of the set. A write is not "committed" until it is on a majority of the servers in a set. If a write has not been committed and network partitions or server crashes isolate it from the majority of the set, the write can end up getting rolled back. (It's a bit outside the scope of this tip, but if you're concerned about rollbacks, I wrote a post (*http://www.snailinaturtleneck.com/blog/2011/01/19/how-to-use-replica-set-roll backs/*) describing how to deal with it.)

w controls the number of servers that a response should be written to before returning success. The way this works is that you issue `getlasterror` to the server (usually just by setting w for a given write operation). The server notes where it is in its oplog ("I'm at operation 123") and then waits for w-1 slaves to have applied operation 123 to their data set. As each slave writes the given operation, w is decremented on the master. Once w is 0, `getlasterror` returns success.

Note that, because the replication always writes operations in order, various servers in your set might be at different "points in history," but they will never have an *inconsistent* data set. They will be identical to the master a minute ago, a few seconds ago, a week ago, etc. They will not be missing random operations.

This means that you can always make sure *num*-1 slaves are synced up to the master by running:

```
> db.runCommand({"getlasterror" : 1, "w" : num})
```

So, the question from an application developer's point-of-view is: what do I set w to? As mentioned above, you need a majority of the set for a write to truly be "safe." However, writing to a minority of the set can also have its uses.

If w is set to a minority of servers, it's easier to accomplish and may be "good enough." If this minority is segregated from the set through network partition or server failure, the majority of the set could elect a new primary and not see the operation that was faithfully replicated to w servers. However, if even one of the members that received the write was not segregated, the other members of the set would sync up to that write before electing a new master.

If w is set to a majority of servers and some network partition occurs or some servers go down, a new master will not be able to be elected without this write. This is a powerful guarantee, but it comes at the cost of w being less likely to succeed: the more servers needed for success, the less likely the success.

Tip #35: Always use wtimeout with w

Suppose you have a three-member replica set (one primary and two secondaries) and want to make sure that your two slaves are up-to-date with the master, so you run:

```
> db.runCommand({"getlasterror" : 1, "w" : 2})
```

But what if one of your secondaries is down? MongoDB doesn't sanity-check the number of secondaries you put: it'll happily wait until it can replicate to 2, 20, or 200 slaves (if that's what w was).

Thus, you should always run `getlasterror` with the `wtimeout` option set to a sensible value for your application. `wtimeout` gives the number of milliseconds to wait for slaves to report back and then fails. This example would wait 100 milliseconds:

```
> db.runCommand({"getlasterror" : 1, "w" : 2, "wtimeout" : 100})
```

Note that MongoDB applies replicated operations in order: if you do writes *A*, *B*, and *C* on the master, these will be replicated to the slave as *A*, then *B*, then *C*. Suppose you have the situation pictured in Figure 4-3. If you do write *N* on master and call `getlasterror`, the slave must replicate writes *E-N* before `getlasterror` can report success. Thus, `getlasterror` can significantly slow your application if you have slaves that are behind.

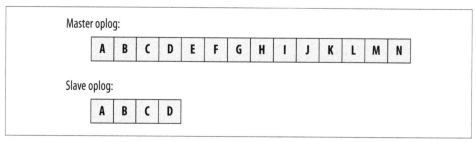

Figure 4-3. A master's and slave's oplogs. The slave's oplog is 10 operations behind the master's.

Another issue is how to program your application to handle `getlasterror` timing out, which is only a question that only you can answer. Obviously, if you are guaranteeing replication to another server, this write is pretty important: what do you do if the write succeeds locally, but fails to replicate to enough machines?

Tip #36: Don't use fsync on every write

If you have important data that you want to ensure makes it to the journal, you must use the `fsync` option when you do a write. `fsync` waits for the next flush (that is, up to 100ms) for the data to be successfully written to the journal before returning success. It is important to note that `fsync` *does not immediately flush data to disk*, it just puts your program on hold until the data has been flushed to disk. Thus, if you run `fsync` on every insert, you will only be able to do one insert per 100ms. This is about a zillion times slower than MongoDB usually does inserts, so use `fsync` sparingly.

`fsync` generally should only be used with journaling. Do not use it when journaling is not enabled unless you're sure you know what you're doing. You can easily hose your performance for absolutely no benefit.

Tip #37: Start up normally after a crash

If you were running with journaling and your system crashes in a recoverable way (i.e., your disk isn't destroyed, the machine isn't underwater, etc.), you can restart the database normally. Make sure you're using all of your normal options, especially --dbpath (so it can find the journal files) and --journal, of course. MongoDB will take care of fixing up your data automatically before it starts accepting connections. This can take a few minutes for large data sets, but it shouldn't be anywhere near the times that people who have run *repair* on large data sets are familiar with (probably five minutes or so).

Journal files are stored in the *journal* directory. *Do not delete these files.*

Tip #38: Take instant-in-time backups of durable servers

To take a backup of a database with journaling enabled, you can either take a filesystem snapshot or do a normal fsync+lock and then dump. Note that you can't just copy all of the files without fsync and locking, as copying is not an instantaneous operation. You might copy the journal at a different point in time than the databases, and then your backup would be worse than useless (your journal files might corrupt your data files when they are applied).

CHAPTER 5

Administration Tips

Tip #39: Manually clean up your chunks collections

GridFS keeps file contents in a collection of chunks, called *fs.chunks* by default. Each document in the files collection points to one or more document in the chunks collection. It's good to check every once and a while and make sure that there are no "orphan" chunks—chunks floating around with no link to a file. This could occur if the database was shut down in the middle of saving a file (the *fs.files* document is written after the chunks).

To check over your chunks collection, choose a time when there's little traffic (as you'll be loading a lot of data into memory) and run something like:

```
> var cursor = db.fs.chunks.find({}, {"_id" : 1, "files_id" : 1});
> while (cursor.hasNext()) {
... var chunk = cursor.next();
... if (db.fs.files.findOne({_id : chunk.files_id}) == null) {
...     print("orphaned chunk: " + chunk._id);
... }
```

This will print out the _ids for all orphaned chunks.

Now, before you go through and delete all of the orphaned chunks, make sure that they are not parts of files that are currently being written! You should check db.curren tOp() and the *fs.files* collection for recent uploadDates.

Tip #40: Compact databases with repair

In "Tip #31: Do not depend on repair to recover data" on page 35, we cover why you usually shouldn't use repair to actually repair your data (unless you're in dire straits). However, repair can be used to compact databases.

Hopefully this tip will become irrelevant soon, once the bug for online compaction is fixed (*http://jira.mongodb.org/browse/SERVER-2120*).

repair basically does a mongodump and then a mongorestore, making a clean copy of your data and, in the process, removing any empty "holes" in your data files. (When you do a lot of deletes or updates that move things around, large parts of your collection could be sitting around empty.) repair re-inserts everything in a compact form.

Remember the caveats to using repair:

- It will block operations, so you don't want to run it on a master. Instead, run it on each secondary first, then finally step down the primary and run it on that server.
- It will take twice the disk space your database is currently using (e.g., if you have 200GB of data, your disk must have at least 200GB of *free space* to run repair).

One problem a lot of people have is that they have too much data to run repair: they might have a 500GB database on a server with 700GB of disk. If you're in this situation, you can do a "manual" repair by doing a mongodump and then a mongorestore.

For example, suppose we have a server that's filling up with mostly empty space at *ny1*. The database is 300GB and the server it's on only has a 400GB disk. However, we also have *ny2*, which is an identical 400GB machine with nothing on it yet. First, we step down *ny1*, if it is master, and fsync and lock it so that there's a consistent view of its data on disk:

```
> rs.stepDown()
> db.runCommand({fsync : 1, lock : 1})
```

We can log into *ny2* and run:

```
ny2$ mongodump --host ny1
```

This will dump the database to a directory called *dump* on *ny2*.

mongodump will probably be constrained by network speed in the above operation. If you have physical access to the machine, plug in an external hard drive and do a local mongodump to that.

Once you have a dump you have to restore it to *ny1*:

1. Shut down the *mongod* running on *ny1*.
2. Back up the data files on *ny1* (e.g., take an EBS snapshot), just in case.
3. Delete the data files on *ny1*.
4. Restart the (now empty) *ny1*. If it was part of a replica set, start it up on a different port and without --replSet, so that it (and the rest of the set) doesn't get confused.

Finally, run mongorestore from *ny2*:

```
ny2$ mongorestore --host ny1 --port 10000 # specify port if it's not 27017
```

Now *ny1* will have a compacted form of the database files and you can restart it with its normal options.

Tip #41: Don't change the number of votes for members of a replica set

If you're looking for a way to indicate preference for mastership, you're looking for priority. In 1.9.0, you can set the priority of a member to be higher than the other members' priorities and it will always be favored in becoming primary. In versions prior to 1.9.0, you can only use priority 1 (can become master) and priority 0 (can't become master). If you are looking to ensure one server always becomes primary, you can't (pre-1.9.0) without giving all of the other servers a priority of 0.

People often anthropomorphize the database and assume that increasing the number of votes a server has will make it win the election. However, servers aren't "selfish" and don't necessarily vote for themselves! A member of a replica set is unselfish and will just as readily vote for its neighbor as it will itself.

Tip #42: Replica sets can be reconfigured without a master up

If you have a minority of the replica set up but the other servers are gone for good, the official protocol is to blow away the *local* database and reconfigure the set from scratch. This is OK for many cases, but it means that you'll have some downtime while you're rebuilding your set and reallocating your oplogs. If you want to keep your application up (although it'll be read-only, as there's no master), you can do it, as long as you have more than one slave still up.

Choose a slave to work with. Shut down this slave and restart it on a different port without the `--replSet` option. For example, if you were starting it with these options:

```
$ mongod --replSet foo --port 5555
```

You could restart it with:

```
$ mongod --port 5556
```

Now it will not be recognized as a member of the set by the other members (because they'll be looking for it on a different port) and it won't be trying to use its replica set configuration (because you didn't tell it that it was a member of a replica set). It is, at the moment, just a normal *mongod* server.

Now we're going to change its replica set configuration, so connect to this server with the shell. Switch to the *local* database and save the replica set configuration to a Java-Script variable. For example, if we had a four-node replica set, it might look something like this:

```
> use local
> config = db.system.replset.findOne()
{
    "_id" : "foo",
    "version" : 2,
    "members" : [
        {
            "_id" : 0,
            "host" : "rs1:5555"
        },
        {
            "_id" : 1,
            "host" : "rs2:5555",
            "arbiterOnly" : true
        },
        {
            "_id" : 2,
            "host" : "rs3:5555"
        },
        {
            "_id" : 3,
            "host" : "rs4:5555"
        }
    ]
}
```

To change our configuration, we need to change the config object to our desired configuration and mark it as "newer" than the configuration that the other servers have, so that they will pick up the change.

The config above is for a four-member replica set, but suppose we wanted to change that to a 3-member replica set, consisting of hosts *rs1*, *rs2*, and *rs4*. To accomplish this, we need to remove the *rs3* element of the array, which can be done using JavaScript's slice function:

```
> config.slice(2, 1)
> config{
    "_id" : "foo",
    "version" : 2,
    "members" : [
        {
            "_id" : 0,
            "host" : "rs1:5555"
        },
        {
            "_id" : 1,
            "host" : "rs2:5555",
            "arbiterOnly" : true
        },
        {
            "_id" : 3,
            "host" : "rs4:5555"
        }
    ]
}
```

Make sure that you do not change *rs4*'s `_id` to 2. This will confuse the replica set. If you are adding new nodes to the set, use JavaScript's `push` function to add elements with `_ids` 4, 5, etc. If you are both adding and removing nodes, you can dive into the confusion that is the JavaScript `splice` function (or you can just use `push` and `slice`).

Now increment the version number (`config.version`). This tells the other servers that this is the new configuration and they should update themselves accordingly.

Now triple-check over your config document. *If you mess up the config, you can completely hose your replica set configuration.* To be clear: nothing bad will happen to your data, but you may have to shut everything down and blow away the *local* database on all of the servers. So make sure this config references the correct servers, no one's `_id` has changed out from under them, and you haven't made any non-arbiters arbiters or visa versa.

Once you're absolutely, completely sure that this is the configuration that you want, shut down the server. Then, restart it with its usual options (`--replSet` and its standard port). In a few seconds, the other member(s) will connect to it, update their configuration, and elect a new master.

Further reading:

- Using `slice` (*http://www.w3schools.com/jsref/jsref_slice_array.asp*)
- Using `push` (*http://www.w3schools.com/jsref/jsref_push.asp*)
- Possible replica set options (*http://www.mongodb.org/display/DOCS/Replica+Set +Configuration#ReplicaSetConfiguration-TheReplicaSetConfigObject*)

Tip #43: --shardsvr and --configsvr aren't required

The documentation seems to imply that these are required when you set up sharding, but they are not. Basically, they just change the port (which can seriously mess up an existing replica set): `--shardsvr` changes the port to 27018 and `--configsvr` changes it to 27019. If you are setting up multiple servers across multiple machines, this is to help you connect the right things together: all *mongos* processes on 27017, all shards on 27018, all config servers on 27019. This setup does make everything a lot easier to keep track of if you're building a cluster from scratch, but don't worry too much about it if you have an existing replica set that you're turning into a shard.

`--configsvr` not only changes the default port but turns on the *diaglog*, a log that keeps every action the config database performs in a replayable format, just in case. If you're using version 1.6, you should use `--port 27019` and `--diaglog`, as `--configsvr` only turns on the diaglog in 1.6.5+. If you're using 1.8, use `--port 27019` and `--journal` (instead of `--diaglog`). Journaling gives you much the same effect as the diaglog with less of a performance hit.

Tip #44: Only use --notablescan in development

MongoDB has an option, `--notablescan`, that returns an error when a query would have to do a table scan (queries that use indexes are processed normally). This can be handy in development if you want to make sure that all of your queries are hitting indexes, but do not use it in production. The problem is that many simple admin tasks require table scans. If you are running MongoDB with `--notablescan` and want to see a list of collections in your database, too bad, that takes a table scan. Want to do some administrative updates based on fields that aren't indexed? Tough, no table scans allowed.

`--notablescan` is a good debugging tool, but it's usually extremely impractical to do *only* indexed queries.

Tip #45: Learn some JavaScript

Even if you are using a language with it's own excellent shell (e.g., Python) or an ODM that abstracts your application away from direct contact with MongoDB (e.g., Mongoid), you should be familiar with the JavaScript shell. It is the quickest, best way of accessing information quickly and a common language among all MongoDB developers.

To get everything possible out of the shell, it helps to know some JavaScript. The following tips go over some features of the language that are often helpful, but there are many others that you might want to use. There are tons of free resources on the Internet and, if you like books (and I'm guessing that you do, if you're reading this one), you might want to pick up *JavaScript: The Good Parts* (*http://oreilly.com/catalog/9780596517748*) (O'Reilly) which is much thinner and more accessible than *JavaScript: The Definitive Guide* (*http://oreilly.com/catalog/9780596101992/*) (also good, but 700 pages longer). I could not possibly hit on every useful feature of JavaScript, but it is a very flexible and powerful language.

Tip #46: Manage all of your servers and databases from one shell

By default, *mongo* connects to *localhost:27017*. You can connect to any server on startup by running *mongo host:port/database*. You can also connect to multiple servers or databases within the shell.

For example, suppose we have an application that has two databases: one *customers* database and one *game* database. If you were working with both, you could keep switching between the two with `use customers`, `use game`, `use customers`, and so on. However, you can also just use separate variables for separate databases:

```
> db
test
```

```
> customers = db.getSisterDB("customers")
customers
> game = db.getSisterDB("game")
game
```

Now you can use them in the same way you'd use db: `game.players.find()`, `custom ers.europe.update()`, etc.

You can also connect db, or any other variable, to another server:

```
> db = connect("ny1a:27017/foo")
connecting to: ny1a:27017/foo
foo
> db
foo
```

This can be particularly handy if you are running a replica set or sharded cluster and you want to connect to more than one node. You could maintain separate connections to the master and slave in your shell:

```
> master = connect("ny1a:27017/admin")
connecting to: ny1a:27017/admin
admin
> slave = connect("ny1b:27017/admin")
connecting to: ny1b:27017/admin
admin
```

You can also connect directly to shards, config servers, or any MongoDB server you have running.

Some shell functions, notably the rs helpers, assume you're using db as your database. If db is connected to a slave or arbiter, some helpers won't work.

One annoyance with connecting to multiple servers through the shell is that MongoDB keeps track of all of the connections you've ever made and, if one goes down, will complain incessantly about it until you bring the server back up or restart the shell. Even undefining the connection doesn't reset this! This will be fixed in version 1.9, but it is currently harmless but noisy.

Tip #47: Get "help" for any function

JavaScript lets you see the source code for most of the functions you run in the shell. If you're curious as to what arguments a function takes or can't remember what it returns, you can see the source by running the function name, without parentheses. For example, suppose we remember that `db.addUser` adds a user, but we can't remember exactly what the arguments are:

```
> db.addUser
function (username, pass, readOnly) {
    readOnly = readOnly || false;
```

```
        var c = this.getCollection("system.users");
        var u = c.findOne({user: username}) || {user: username};
        u.readOnly = readOnly;
        u.pwd = hex_md5(username + (":mongo:" + pass));
        print(tojson(u));
        c.save(u);
    }
```

We can see immediately that we give it a username, password, and that there's a readOnly option (to create a user who can only read from the given database).

Also note that you can see the JavaScript API online (*http://api.mongodb.org/js*). The online "documentation" is not actually very well documented, but it is a complete reference of the functions available.

There is also quite a bit of built-in help for commands. If you can't remember the command you want to run, you can see them all as long as you remember one: the listCommands command! This shows you the name of each command:

```
> db.runCommand({listCommands : 1})
{
    "commands" : {
        "_isSelf" : { ... },
        ...
    }
    "ok" : 1
}
```

If you have the command name, you can get some built-in documentation on it from the database by running {*commandName* : 1, help : 1} (even if the command wouldn't normally have 1 after its name). This will display some basic documentation that the database has about each command, which varies from very helpful to barely English:

```
> db.runCommand({collstats : 1, help : 1})
{
    "help" : "help for: collStats { collStats: "blog.posts" , scale : 1 }
        scale divides sizes e.g. for KB use 1024",
    "lockType" : -1,
    "ok" : 1
}
```

The shell also has tab completion, so you can get suggestions of what to type next based on the functions, fields, and even collections that exist:

```
> db.c
db.cloneCollection(    db.constructor        db.currentOP(
db.cloneDatabase(      db.copyDatabase(      db.currentOp(
db.commandHelp(        db.createCollection(
> db.copyDatabase()
```

As of this writing, shell completion only works on *NIX systems.

Tip #48: Create startup files

You can optionally run a startup file (or files) when the shell starts. A startup file is usually a list of user-defined helper functions, but it is simply a JavaScript program. To make one, create a file with a *.js* suffix (say, *startup.js*) and start *mongo* with mongo startup.js.

For example, suppose you are doing some shell maintenance and you don't want to accidentally drop a database or remove records. You can remove some of the less-safe commands in the shell (e.g., database and collection dropping, removing documents, etc.):

```
// no-delete.js

delete DBCollection.prototype.drop;
delete DBCollection.prototype.remove;
delete DB.prototype.dropDatabase;
```

Now, if you tried to drop a collection, *mongo* would not recognize the function:

```
$ mongo no-delete.js
MongoDB shell version: 1.8.0
connecting to: test
> db.foo.drop()
Wed Feb 16 14:24:16 TypeError: db.foo.drop is not a function (shell):1
```

This is only to prevent a user from hamfisting away data: it offers zero protection from a user who knows what they're doing and is determined to drop the collection. Deleting functions should not be used as security against malicious attacks (because it gives you none), only to prevent blunders.

 If someone was really determined to drop the collection and drop() was gone, they could simply run db.$cmd.findOne({drop : "foo"}). You cannot prevent this without deleting find(), which would make the shell essentially useless.

You could create a fairly extensive list of blacklisted functions, depending on what you wanted to prevent (index creation, running database commands, etc.) You can specify as many of these files as you want when *mongo* is started, so you could modularize these, too.

Tip #49: Add your own functions

If you'd like to add your own functions, you can define and use them by adding them as global functions, to instances of a class, or to the class itself (meaning every instance of the class will have an instance of the function).

For example, suppose we are using "Tip #46: Manage all of your servers and databases from one shell" on page 46 to connect to every member of a replica set and we want to add a getOplogLength function.

If we think of this before we get started, we could add it to the database class (DB):

```
DB.prototype.getOplogLength = function() {
    var local = this.getSisterDB("local");
    var first = local.oplog.rs.find().sort({$natural : 1}).limit(1).next();
    var last = local.oplog.rs.find().sort({$natural : -1}).limit(1).next();
    print("total time: " + (last.ts.t - first.ts.t) + " secs");
};
```

Then, when we connect to *rsA*, *rsB*, and *rsC* databases, each will have a getOplogSize method.

If we've already started using *rsA*, *rsB*, and *rsC*, then they won't pick up that you added a new method to the class that they came from (classes in JavaScript are sort of like templates for class instances: the instance has no dependency on the class once it's initialized). If the connections have already been initialized, you can add this method to each instance:

```
// store the function in a variable to save typing
var f = function() { ... }
rsA.getOplogSize = f;
rsB.getOplogSize = f;
rsC.getOplogSize = f;
```

You could also just alter it slightly to be a global function:

```
getOplogLength = function(db) {
    var local = db.getSisterDB("local");
    ...
};
```

You can, of course, also do this for an object's fields (as well as its methods).

Loading JavaScript from files

You can add JavaScript libraries to your shell at any time using the load() function. load() takes a JavaScript file and executes it in the context of the shell (so it will know about all of the global variables in the shell). You can also add variables to the shell's global scope by defining them in loaded files. You can also print output from these files to the shell using the print function:

```
// hello.js

print("Hello, world!")
```

Then, in the shell:

```
> load("hello.js")
Hello, world!
```

One of the most common queries about replica sets and sharding is from ops people who want to be able to set them up from a configuration file. You must set up replica sets and sharding programmatically, but you could write out the setup functions in a JavaScript file which you could execute to set up the set. It's close to being able to use a configuration file.

Tip #50: Use a single connection to read your own writes

When you create a connection to a MongoDB server, this connection behaves like a queue for requests. So, for example, if you send messages A, B, and then C to the database through this connection, MongoDB will process message A, then message B, then message C. That is not a guarantee that each operation would succeed: A could be the shutdownServer command and then B and C would return errors (if they were messages that expected replies at all). However, you do have the guarantee that they will be sent and processed in order (see Figure 5-1).

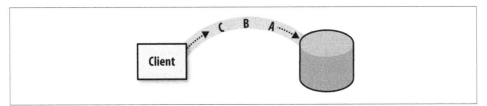

Figure 5-1. A connection to MongoDB is like a queue.

This is useful: suppose you increment the number of downloads for a product and do a findOne on that product: you expect to see the incremented number of downloads. However, if you're using more than one connection (and most drivers use a pool of connections automatically), you might not.

Suppose that you have two connections to the database (from the same client). Each of the connections will be sending messages that will be processed in serial, but there is no guarantee of order across the connections: if the first connection sends messages A, B, and C and the second sends D, E, and F, the messages might be processed as A, D, B, E, C, F or A, B, C, D, E, F, or any other merge of the two sequences (see Figure 5-2).

If A is inserting a new document and D is querying for that document, D might end up going first (say, D, A, E, B, F, C) and, thus, not find the record. To fix this, drivers with connection pooling generally have a way of specifying that a group of requests should be sent on the same connection to prevent this "read your own write" discrepancy. Other drivers will do this automatically (using a single connection from the pool per "session"), check your driver's documentation for details.

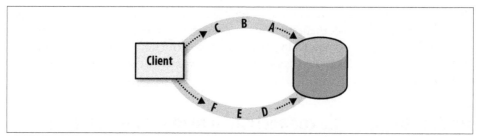

Figure 5-2. Individual connections will send requests in order, but requests from different connections may be interleaved.

Get even more for your money.

Join the O'Reilly Community, and register the O'Reilly books you own. It's free, and you'll get:

- $4.99 ebook upgrade offer
- 40% upgrade offer on O'Reilly print books
- Membership discounts on books and events
- Free lifetime updates to ebooks and videos
- Multiple ebook formats, DRM FREE
- Participation in the O'Reilly community
- Newsletters
- Account management
- 100% Satisfaction Guarantee

Signing up is easy:

1. **Go to: oreilly.com/go/register**
2. **Create an O'Reilly login.**
3. **Provide your address.**
4. **Register your books.**

Note: English-language books only

To order books online:
oreilly.com/store

For questions about products or an order:
orders@oreilly.com

To sign up to get topic-specific email announcements and/or news about upcoming books, conferences, special offers, and new technologies:
elists@oreilly.com

For technical questions about book content:
booktech@oreilly.com

To submit new book proposals to our editors:
proposals@oreilly.com

O'Reilly books are available in multiple DRM-free ebook formats. For more information:
oreilly.com/ebooks

O'REILLY®

Spreading the knowledge of innovators   oreilly.com

The information you need, when and where you need it.

With Safari Books Online, you can:

Access the contents of thousands of technology and business books

- Quickly search over 7000 books and certification guides
- Download whole books or chapters in PDF format, at no extra cost, to print or read on the go
- Copy and paste code
- Save up to 35% on O'Reilly print books
- **New!** Access mobile-friendly books directly from cell phones and mobile devices

Stay up-to-date on emerging topics before the books are published

- Get on-demand access to evolving manuscripts.
- Interact directly with authors of upcoming books

Explore thousands of hours of video on technology and design topics

- Learn from expert video tutorials
- Watch and replay recorded conference sessions

Spreading the knowledge of innovators   safari.oreilly.com

Lightning Source UK Ltd.
Milton Keynes UK
UKHW031332170921
390741UK00007B/185